Hadrian's Cycleway

&

Coast 2 Coast

ISBN: 9781089501954

Cover design by Dave Lewis

Photographs by Dave Lewis, Sue Gurman, Eve Phoebe Lewis

Also available as an e-book

For more information contact the author:
www.david-lewis.co.uk

Published in the UK by www.publishandprint.co.uk

Special thanks to:
Sue, Eve and Lili for driving me to Cumbria, following me around, providing moral support and a wet nose

Dave Lewis

---

*Hadrian's Cycleway
&
Coast 2 Coast*

Publish & Print
www.publishandprint.co.uk

For Sue, Eve & Lili

'Over the heather the wet wind blows,
I've lice in my tunic and a cold in my nose.

The rain comes pattering out of the sky,
I'm a Wall soldier, I don't know why.

The mist creeps over the hard grey stone,
My girl's in Tungria; I sleep alone.

Aulus goes hanging around her place,
I don't like his manners, I don't like his face.

Piso's a Christian, he worships a fish;
There'd be no kissing if he had his wish.

She gave me a ring but I diced it away;
I want my girl and I want my pay.

When I'm a veteran with only one eye
I shall do nothing but look at the sky.'

- WH Auden

Contents

Roman Holiday

'Ah! Gentle, fleeting, wav'ring sprite,
Friend and associate of this clay!'
- Hadrian

Trust me to want to cycle backwards. Especially as on my last two 'big' trips I'd managed to go with the wind. And of course if you read any UK cycling guidebooks or websites they will all tell you to go west to east or south to north. If you're looking at Land's End to John o' Groats (LEJOG) cycle uphill (north) and if you're going to do the Coast to Coast / Sea to Sea (C2C) route across northern England then go east young man! The hill gradients are easier and the prevailing winds ease your passage. Bugger!

It was my own fault of course. After the success of setting up the *'Wales Trails'* route, where I'd designed the snazzy website – www.wales-trails.co.uk, enjoyed the very modest but pleasing book sales, raised over £500 for Prostate Cancer Wales and hopefully put the land of my father on the world cycling map I had the bug again. The cycling bug I mean, not my old friend double pneumonia, which was never far away either.

I'd always wanted to ride across the north of England, especially the scenic Lake District, Celtic Cumbria and perhaps do the famous C2C route. It was, after all, the most popular *long-ish* distance, cycle ride in the UK. Not as famous as LEJOG but it was up there. The problem was, whilst looking at the map, I'd also discovered the Hadrian's Cycleway. This is a route that roughly follows the old Roman wall built by Emperor Hadrian. Well, when I say 'built by' I doubt whether the old guy actually laid any of the bricks himself and he died before it was completed anyway. In fact three legions of infantrymen took around six years to complete the construction. Each legion was around 5,000 men strong and extra manpower was provided by conquered tribes. I think we call them slaves nowadays.

Anyway, now I wanted to do two rides. The C2C and the Hadrian's Cycleway. OK, first problem. Both routes should really be cycled west to east for the reasons given earlier but I wasn't sure I'd have the time to do two separate rides that were so far from my home town in Pontypridd, south Wales.

Starting point at Ravenglass, Cumbria

Right, easy solution, I'll combine them and do both. And so yet another silly plan was born. I'd make it a loop and embrace the Buddhist doctrine of doing stuff in a clockwise direction. I'd start one end and cycle around Cumbria and Northumberland, taking in some great Roman towns, see a bit of the famous wall, have a '*Newky Brown*' in Newcastle, see the river and iconic bridge (designed and built by the same contractors that built the Sydney Harbour Bridge), visit the mouth of the Tyne, tunnel or ferry across (whichever was open / running), pop down to Sunderland, then cross-country, over the Pennines, wind my way through the Lake District, over some horrible hills (or try to avoid them) and down to the beach for a couple of beers while watching *'Game of Thrones'* or *'Gladiator'* or some such suitable swords and toga epic on the B&B TV. Probably *'Carry On Cleo'* with my luck.

Not a bad plan I thought and seeing as I'd probably be biking alone again I thought it best to at least look at Google Maps or something before I went up north. Then I stumbled upon more problems. What shall I call this trip / book? Do I wear a centurion's helmet or a cloth cap that might have been worn by the great poet Wordsworth? Oh dear, too many choices.

Then it came to me. I'd call the trip 'Roman Holiday'. A truly inspired idea I thought, until I looked on Amazon for cycling books called 'Roman Holiday'. Mmm? None. OK, rethink...

*

Like Audrey Hepburn in the film *'Roman Holiday'* I was becoming frustrated with my slightly disjointed, self-employed routine, the constant demands on my time when I was supposed to be working from home.

"Dad, can you give me a lift to the farm, I want to ride Milly, Nick's racehorse." Or my mam who wants to buy melons from Sainsbury's, or visits to the vets with the dog, or a quick drive to Greg's pub to pick something up... the list is endless.

So rather than wait another eleven years (like I did between LEJOG and Wales Trails) I thought why not cycle somewhere this summer. I needed a break and this idea would work fine.

That was back in early 2017 mind you, when I had the idea and first started to plan a route. I'd booked a number of Airbnbs and even had the offer of company from my mate Mark (although this was before his son was singing somewhere after winning the *'Kids Voice'* and making friends with Pixie Lott, whoever she is).

I even fixed my trusty Dawes; as I knew that the rest of my time on the ride would be spent fixing Mark's bike (him being even worse than me regards maintenance of such machines). There was good news on the health front too. My kidney pain seemed to have settled down after various antibiotics, scans and waiting lists and although I had put back on the weight I'd lost cycling around Wales I still felt fit enough to bimble along a few trails for a week or so. So it was all looking good.

Part of the ancient wall

Then my eighty-five year old mam (who is also called Audrey as it happens) got knocked off her feet during a labradoodle play day I'd organised. Shit. Why do I arrange these things?

Mam shattered her femur pretty bad and so I had to cancel the trip. I texted all the Airbnbs and in fairness they were all great about it (apart from one) and refunded my money. So instead of jumping on a bike that summer I just watched Gregory Peck find a drugged up Princess Audrey on a bench.

OK, fast-forward two years and another twist of fate intervenes when my wife and I decide to buy a second-hand VW campervan.

"It'll be a laugh," says Sue.

"How much?" I wasn't laughing.

And so with a set of wheels that could serve as a state-of-the-art support vehicle I dig out my old maps again and think about planning a touristy trip for Sue, Eve and Lili the dog.

"I hope you like forts and mountains and stuff?" I ask.

"Yeh I suppose, if I can fit it in amongst my hectic social schedule," replies my daughter, who is a little annoyed we spent the last of our savings on an old motorhome rather than a safari to Zambia and Malawi.

So just like the character 'Ann' in the famous film we decide we'll have a *'Roman Holiday'* ourselves albeit in Cumbria rather than *'Rome! By all means, Rome.'*

OK, time for the history bit.

*

The Roman conquest of Britain was a gradual process; beginning effectively in 43 AD under Emperor Claudius and continuing for almost 400 years before the Romans finally got fed up with crowd control and left us to fight amongst ourselves.

The British language at the time of the invasion was Common Brittonic, and remained so after the Romans withdrew. It later split into regional languages, notably Cumbric, Cornish, Breton and Welsh although 800 Latin words were incorporated into Common Brittonic as well. The English language is based on the languages of the Germanic tribes who migrated to the island from continental Europe from the 5th Century onwards.

Right what about this wall then? Well, the defensive fortification was begun in 122 AD by Emperor Hadrian. It went right across northern England, from the banks of the River Tyne near the North Sea to Solway Firth in the Irish Sea. It represented the northern most part of the UK that the Romans felt they were able to control. Above the wall were the ancient Britons who were a pretty mad bunch.

Hadrian's Wall, Birdoswald

The original stone wall had seventeen forts plus eighty milecastles, where garrisons of soldiers would live. Although not that much of the original structure still remains Hadrian's Wall is one of the largest Roman artefacts remaining anywhere in the world. Having said that, 91% has gone but there is still enough left for the wall to have been given UNESCO World Heritage Site status in 1987.

There is a misconception that the wall represents the border between England and Scotland. All of the wall is actually inside English territory, a mile inside at Bowness-on-Solway and sixty-eight miles inside on the east coast.

Back in the day the wall was covered in plaster and

painted white. It's shining surface, on the rare days the sun shines this far north, would have meant it was visible for miles around and a potent symbol of Roman power.

After Hadrian's death the new emperor, Antonius Pius abandoned the wall and built his own version, much further north. The Antonine Wall was only about forty miles long but as he failed to conquer the tribes up there, when Marcus Aurelius became emperor he left it to the Scots and reoccupied Hadrian's Wall instead. Clever chap old Marcus.

When the Romans eventually gave up on trying to civilise us barbarians and went back to their grapes and orgies the wall, with its collection of turrets, forts and small castles were immediately occupied by the Britons but soon the wall fell into disrepair and people just used the stone to build their own houses. What are we like eh?

Today the wall is a tourist attraction and remains unguarded or unfenced, which means people can climb all over it and damage it. In 2003 a National Trust footpath was opened which follows the line of the wall. The cycle path was officially opened in July 2006.

Planning

If you've read my other two cycling accounts you probably realise that planning isn't my favourite bit. Mainly because like the old Robert Burns adage, 'the best-laid plans of mice and men often go awry'. So whilst I like to be prepared to a certain extent I know that life happens when you're making other plans and so apart from printing off some maps and a list of places to camp or park up the campervan it seemed best to just turn up and see what happens.

Of course with this ride there was one big difference. I had a support vehicle and technically somewhere to kip if I had to stop short of my desired destination on any given day. The VW campervan was hopefully going to come into its own and with my wife Sue driving, my daughter and dog along for the 'ride' too it was always going to be a cycling trip with a difference. A real family affair.

The basic plan was to stock up the van with dog food, a bike rack and head north from Wales after Sue finished work on a Friday afternoon. We'd drive as far as we could; van, traffic, light willing and then find somewhere to pitch up and bed down for the night. Then next morning, quick breakie and drive to the lakes and across to Ravenglass where I hoped to jump on the bike and stretch my cycling legs.

I did think about a guidebook, but not for long. They're bound to have signs with Roman shields or something I figured and I'd just follow them. What could go wrong?

I checked the routes online and was informed they were suitable for road bikes along almost all of the sections. That'll do for me I thought. The revamped Dawes Discovery 701 will do nicely. I'll pack the same kit as I did for 'Wales Trails', use the new panniers I bought for that trip and take a couple of spare inner tubes. What could possibly go wrong? Oh dear, I remember just saying that.

OK, I now had to work out how far I would be cycling

and how many days it would take me. I didn't want to be away for too long but reckoned a week should be plenty of time to complete both routes, one east and the other west.

The Challenge – I'd start at Ravensglass and do Hadrian's Cycleway to Sunderland (192 miles in four days), then do Sunderland to Whitehaven (134 miles in three days). I calculated the total distance (if all went well) would be approximately 326 miles.

Kit – I would use my trust / rusty / untrusty (delete as applicable) Dawes with proper wheels and take two small panniers to carry a few essentials (see full kit list below). Of course the advantage of having the van was I could bring a proper pump and hopefully, mobile signal willing, I'd only be a phone call from rescue if need be.

Digs – being only a few less book sales away from the food bank I decided we couldn't really afford to B&B it for a whole week so started to research some bunkhouses and dorms to compliment the campsites we'd use with the van. Ah, first problem. I couldn't really find any on the route. They were all a bit off the route. Out in the wilderness in fact. Ah well, van it is then! I'd have to shower (bath) in a stream.

There would also be another slight variation on my previous cycling trips, where I'd always booked a nice comfy bed with hot bath to soak the aching limbs. Yes the camper van was convenient, especially for carrying extra stuff but as my daughter was coming along too it meant I was relegated to the tiny, one-man tent and would be camping outside the nice warm van. Even the dog would be inside!

Training – as all tip-top bikers will tell you, training is crucial. And having struggled quite a bit on my last adventure I decided it best to not even think about it at all this time. It

9

might bring back horrible memories and I wouldn't go.

I did dust the bike down and go for one training ride but unfortunately my wife Sue only agreed to let me go if we could have a new decking. I agreed but forgot about the impact of filling the basement shed with everything from the old decking; chairs, plants, Buddhas and stuff. My bikes were now buried under a multitude of metal, pot plants and spiritualism. Oops! Ah well, I'd do my training on the way as always.

Diet – the ride around Wales turned out to be a great way to lose weight, gain a six-pack (thirty years after I lost it under a bellyful of beer) and get compliments from women that I didn't realise thought I was a fat bastard before I lost the weight!

So a week of chippies, curry and real ale it would be – horray! I really should write a diet book. I had lost a stone last year and quickly put it back on again so here was my chance to undo all the bad and slim down to under 100kg again.

I'd also recently discovered Aldi's 'Hike' bars; with 21g of protein, so decided to take a dozen of them for mid-morning / afternoon snacks to slot between my greasy fry-ups, mid-day 'Meal Deals' of sandwich, crisps and Lucozade, and my main evening pig-out before I had a couple of pints to help me sleep and carbo-load for the following day. Fermented vegetable juice is carbohydrate isn't it?

Aches & Pains – during 2016 I did have a few sleepless nights thanks to having some sort of kidney complaint. At first I thought it was my back so just did a few side-bends / twists in the morning to 'click' it back into place. Unfortunately it wasn't until I was home, still in agony, that someone suggested kidney stones. I booked an appointment with the GP, had a couple of visits, an ultrasound scan and eventually a CT scan…

"If you were a horse they'd shoot you," said my mate Mark reassuringly.

Weird thing was the quacks didn't really find anything, which I think is good?

Anyway, age being what it is. I had a lovely groin strain (from footie), a sprayed wrist (either gym or RSI from typing stuff), a sore neck (from almost breaking it after somersaulting off my mountain bike a few years back as well as years of rugby) and some arthritis in my foot (after breaking it, not realising it was broke and hopping around Poland on a stag weekend) but other than that I was in tip-top condition! Actually my lower back was killing me but I've had that for years.

Transport – for the LEJOG tour (back in 2005) my wife Sue had driven me and Derek to Land's End whilst friends Mark and Alun had driven up to meet us in John o' Groats. For the Welsh loop I'd started and finished at the house but this trip was miles away again. Normally I'd require a lift. Two lifts in fact – one to the start and one to pick me up at the end but...

Enter the VW Transporter campervan conversion. Fingers crossed the answer to all our cycling logistics problems for the next few years.

"Sue, fancy a night in the Lake District? Eve can come, she's never been there..."

"Oh that sounds nice."

"Great, I'll oil my bike."

"What?"

"And you'll be able to visit Newcastle, see the bridge and stuff."

"What about the dog?"

"She can come too."

"And how far are you planning on cycling this time?"

"Not far, about three hundred ish."

"Bloody hell."

And so it went. It's a long drive from south Wales to Cumbria, especially taking it easy with the van and bike stuck on the back. I estimated six hours plus stops so we decided to leave the night before to try to miss the Cardiff, Newport, Birmingham, Manchester etc. rush hours. It was a sort of plan anyway.

Weather - doing the trip in August we were bound to get some decent weather, lol, but just in case I even DuckDuckGo'd that.

Here was the forecast for Newcastle just before we left:

Don't you just love the great outdoors in the UK! Warm and wet. Well at least it was warm.

Charity – it was all a bit of a rush in the end, Boris and the Tories were probably going to push for a no-deal Brexit, sell off the NHS to Trump and so if all us poor people were going to die I thought it prudent to allow my family and friends to keep their money for a little longer, until they really needed it, rather than line the pockets of some charity CEO who earns £100k+.

Kit List

X1 Bike – Dawes Discovery 701 – great bike (just read the 'Land's End to John o' Groats' book if you don't believe me), new wheels and tyres (see 'Wales Trails' book).

X1 Helmet – Bell model (Halfords), which I bought after the last one split in two whilst saving my life when I fell off cycling up and down Sugar Loaf mountain in Abergavenny. I mention this fact because apparently if you have an accident and the helmet saves you then Bell will give you a new one for free – worth knowing!

X2 Spare inner tubes – Halfords (cheaper)

X1 Puncture repair kit (with those impossible to use tyre levers)

X3 pairs of surgical rubber gloves (for oily chain stuff)

X1 small pack of wet-wipes

X1 Multipurpose spanner, set of Allen keys, spoke tightener

X1 Bike lock

X1 small Dual action pump (with small gauge)

X1 Pannier rack with two small Arran panniers (one with a friendship bracelet tied to the zip so I knew which one had my ointments and magical balms in)

X2 Water bottles

X1 Bike computer – Garmin Edge 200 (plug and charger)

X1 Cycling top (a walking, base layer from Trespass)

X1 T-shirt with 'Wales Trails' logo on to advertise previous cycling book / adventure (never miss a chance to market!)

X2 cboardman gel cycling shorts (only x1 pair actually fitted me though)

X2 Pairs walking socks – Jeep (x3 pairs for £8 in T.k.maxx)

X1 Merrell Tahr Bolt waterproof hiking shoes. Fed up of cold, wet feet last time so thought this time I'd just have cold, wet socks

X1 Waterproof jacket (just about showerproof anyway)

X1 Cycling gloves – Aldi (fingerless, from Crane)

X1 Sealskin gloves (long-fingered, a spare pair in case it got cold when the 'American Werewolf in London' was chasing me over the moors, excuse my poor geography)

X3 Pants – one on, one off, one for Sunday best

X2 T-shirts – for pub in night (took two 'cos I'm very fashion conscious!)

X1 Cargo shorts

X1 Sandals – (Teva) to air the feet

Trying to organise my kit for the week!

X1 Camera – a small compact, waterproof, shockproof, digital camera – Canon Powershot D30 (battery, charger, SD card)

X1 iPhone 5 – for Google Maps when I inevitably got lost. I also added some Romanesque marching music to my iTunes Playlists to get me in the mood each morning. Last trip I took a diary and pen but ended up using the phone's 'Notes' app, which I discovered after I was halfway around Wales. I tried to do the same this trip but as there was no hope my phone battery would hold out for more than a few hours when you actually use the soddin' thing I was glad I had the diray as backup

X1 'Curry card' (i.e. my Visa / cashpoint card) – for beers, sandwiches, border guard bribes, alms to lost Centurions, B&Bs / campsites, cycle repairs, buying 'Meal Deals' in corner shops (this assuming the Romans actually incorporated corners into their walls and roads)

X1 Print out of rough route with hill profiles (I'm getting older now so care about these things), pubs, B&B addresses and telephone numbers

X2 Plastic bags – to put my pants and t-shirts in when it rained (this is the north of England in summer remember)

X1 Shower gel (small)

X1 Toothpaste (small) / brush

X1 Sun cream F30 (small) – joking right!

X1 Toilet roll – in case I got caught short near a fort, turret, milecastle, Roman baths, ditch, vallum, wing wall, berm, glacis, football stadium, mountain, lake, and had to do a Forest Gump in the bushes

Hadrian's Cycleway

'He had reached that moment in life, different for each one of us, when a man abandons himself to his demon or to his genius, following a mysterious law which bids him either to destroy or outdo himself.'
- Hadrian

The route is pretty straightforward. Start at the Glannaventa Roman Bath House in Ravenglass and finish at the Arbeia Roman Fort in South Shields. Total distance is 174 miles although I know I'll do less than that if I can wangle it.

The route follows the National Cycle Network, Route 72 and is a mixture of on road and traffic free. The trails take in Hadrian's Wall World Heritage Site, go from coast to coast across the northern most part of England, taking in great scenery, quaint villages, market towns and modern cities.

Most bikes are suitable and I take my 'road' or touring bike, the now infamous Dawes Discovery 701 (Mk II). I say that because it was mostly rebuilt during 'Wales Trails', but that's another story… (Available from all good book shops).

# Day 1

Pontypridd - Cumbria
Friday 2nd August 2019

Had a fairly lazy day. Up at 8:00am, took the dog for a walk and started to panic about whether I'd packed enough stuff for the trip. You know, the usual worry that you've forgotten something important. Then I thought about my old university mate Wayne. We'd recently learnt that he'd passed away a couple of weeks ago of a heart attack in Australia. Suddenly the ride became nothing. 'So what?' if I hadn't packed the sudocrem or if the weather was going to be shit.

My wife always says, 'Life is for living'. It's a good motto to remember and one I frequently remind myself of, especially, whenever I feel a bit blue, which is quite often these days. Probably as a consequence of my current financial situation, which makes church mice seem like yuppie playboys with all the Cheddar they can stuff into their cheek pouches but that's another story...

After packing the VW T30 Transporter (campervan conversion) with hippie cushions and a mellow collection of CDs, not to mention my bike stuff and everyone's kit I did the dishes. House all tidy – great. Then Greg, Fair and George popped in to cook food. House untidy. Did the dishes and tidied up again. Then Eve did food for herself. More dishes. Took my Mam to the bus stop, then picked Sue up from work. Came home but Eve had just had a pizza. More housework. And people wonder why I'm such a slow worker!

OK, almost set. Last thing to do is attach the bike and we'll be off. I did manage to attach the Aldi's bike rack to the campervan's towbar but then I couldn't get the bike on!

Right, I'm not stupid I thought, I'll work it out. I took off the extra attachments for bikes two and three, which allowed me to squeeze my Dawes frame over the bars. There sorted.

But alas that just made the rack tilt at a funny angle and no matter how tight I screwed the lock it made no difference. Guess I am stupid. Stupid to have believed a cheap £25 bike rack would have worked.

"Bugger!"

"You did check the bike fitted?" demands Sue as our mate Rhys passes.

"Hi Rhys."

"Off cycling Dave?"

"Not if he can't attach his bike we're not," says Sue. "Please say you tested it?"

"Yeh of course I did."

"Are you sure? Well how come it doesn't work now then?"

"Well, it looked alright."

Rhys laughed.

"What? I can't believe you've had months to try it out and now you're saying it won't fit!"

"Aye, it did work fine."

"When did you try it? Actually put the bike on and drive around a bit," asks Sue while Eve giggles.

"Well, I thought it would be OK."

"WTF%&*^£$)*&@..."

"I'll leave you to it then," says Rhys and walks off.

I gave up and just threw the bike in the back of the van, climbed over it to sit down and off Sue drove. On the road by 6:00pm.

We drive down the A470 from 'Ponty' to Cardiff, onto the M4, past Newport and turn north up the M50 for Monmouth and Ross.

We weren't really sure how far we'd get, what with weekend rush hour traffic and a self-imposed speed limit of about fifty mph but we have no hold ups.

It was a beautiful evening and the forecast for the week was pretty good too. Rain for a few days but hopefully just showers I could dodge. We made good time to Worcester before Brum, then we hit roadworks. Why is it in the UK you can't drive anywhere without roadworks? We pushed on until we got to the M6.

Lili and Dawes in the back of the van

What amazed me though was the amount of traffic, even when we got to eight and nine o'clock. We stopped at some services as Eve wanted a McDonalds.

I was a bit peckish too so asked the girl behind the counter for a chicken burger, it cost 99p and I gave her a pound.

I waited but she didn't offer the penny change so I felt the urge to say something.

"Hi, I gave you a pound," I said smiling.

Blank look.

"A penny change?" I offered.

She tutted, said something under her breath about getting the manager to open the till and wandered off.

She gave me the penny with a scowl. Right that was it!

"Only a penny?" I say.

"Yeh?"

"Why not twopence?"

"Wha?"

"Well, you had no problem stealing a penny from me so why not give me a penny too much back?"

Blank look again.

"So it's OK to short change me a penny but you wouldn't dream of giving me an extra penny back?"

I took my burger and left as the girl probably used social media to tell all her friends how horrible Canadians are.

Eve laughed.

Back on the road we pass Lancaster and turn off the M6 towards the 'lakes'. It was very dark and we decided to find a layby to try to get a few hours sleep.

We parked up at about 1:00am, I put the bike on the roof and thought good luck to anyone brave enough to climb up there in the middle of the night to get it.

I manage an hour or so of sleep. Sue too. Eve moans.

It's light by 5:00am so we decide to hit the road again.

Eve is still moaning and threatens to kick me.

"Oh she's such a delight when she's tired," says Sue.

Then she jams the pillows in the cupboard and it won't open properly, followed by...

"My shower gel has leaked everywhere. I want to go home."

We have a cup of tea and some cornflakes and are soon on the road again.

Happy days.

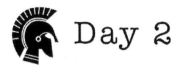

Day 2

Ravenglass to Workington
Saturday 3rd August 2019

iPhone track: Another Brick In The Wall – Pink Floyd

Although we're already awake my iPhone alarm kicks in. Pink Floyd was the best track I could think of to symbolise a 'wall'. If only The Bangles had wanted to 'Cycle Like A Roman' instead of 'Walk Like An Egyptian' I'd have been quids in but there you go.

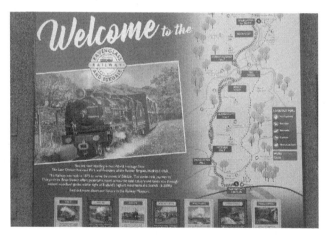

Railway tourist attraction

My back is aching and I haven't even attempted to sit on the saddle and pedal anywhere yet. I try to remember what the guidebook / website says about this part of the country:

21

'A ride through some of England's most dramatic and wild countryside, taking in magnificent coastal views, breathtaking countryside and Roman forts.'

We arrive early in Ravenglass and discover a beautiful little village nestled on the edge of the estuary of three rivers, the Esk, the Mite and the Irt. Ravenglass was an important naval base for the Romans although only the bath house remains these days.

The start of the trip

We park the VW in the pay and display and I get the bike ready for the first leg of my journey. We take a stroll around the Ravenglass and Eskdale Railway, which is now a major tourist attraction. The railway used to serve the mines near Boot, about eight miles away, bringing granite, iron and copper ore to the estuary.

We cross the railway line and walk through the woodland with Lili until we reach the Roman baths. Eve takes a photo and off I go. An easy day today, or at least that's what

I planned, seeing as I was knackered after the drive north plus the lack of sleep in the van.

The country lane takes you back to the village, past the railway and you are soon on a footpath facing the sea. Bigger cyclists (am I allowed to say fat ones like me?) will probably need to push the bike along the paths under the bridge but soon you are across the bay from Ravenglass and on a rough trail next to the beach.

At Holmrook I see a sign for the famous Bridge Inn pub which every November holds the 'World's Biggest Liar' competition to see who can come up with such classic porkies as the giant turnips that could be used as sheds for the Herdwick sheep or the fact that the Lake District wasn't formed by volcanic action but was actually the result of large moles and eels. Good ole Will Ritson. I did think of cycling there but I'd be lying if I said that. Or did I?

Looking ominous behind the golf course

I turn seaward towards Drigg. I cycle uphill but don't linger as there is a nuclear decommissioning site based here where one million cubic metres of radioactive waste is housed, although disposal records are incomplete (very convenient).

The dunes are beautiful though and there are plenty if seabirds around, even if they do look like giant prehistoric auks with huge bloody fangs. I follow an off road path, cycling through sand and then I see it. It's quite scary even though it provides much employment in the area.

Warning sign on fence

Sellafield is a nuclear fuel reprocessing site near the village of Seascale. It is the site of the world's first nuclear power station that generated electricity on an industrial scale. It is of course completely safe and that is why it was located here, about as far away from Westminster, the royal family, the BBC and Eton college as it could be in England.

First constructed during the Second World War (1942) Sellafield (or Windscale as it was later known) started playing with plutonium (one of the most poisonous substances known to man) in 1947.

It has been calculated that one pound of plutonium could kill two million people by inhalation if it were released into the atmosphere. This makes the toxicity of plutonium roughly equivalent with that of nerve gas, so all good then!

In 1957, the Windscale fire, became the worst nuclear accident in UK history and ranked five out of seven on the International Nuclear Event Scale. That is the same as the meltdown at 'Three Mile Island' in 1979 but not as bad as 'Chernobyl' in 1986, which topped the charts at seven.

Train of nuclear waste

I could drone on about Sellafield, lol, but let's just say that the worries about cancer rates near the plant will never go away, no matter how often the government claims it is safe, especially when studies show that levels of plutonium in children's teeth are double normal levels near the facility while other medical studies have shown an increase in childhood leukaemia.

Ireland, Norway and the Isle of Man have all objected to the site. When you hear that in 2005 the UK Atomic Energy Authority reported that nearly thirty kilograms of plutonium was unaccounted for in audits you can't blame them! Very Jason Bourne.

Popular music has also featured the plant with 'Spear of Destiny', 'U2' and 'Kraftwerk' all producing songs about the dangers of the site.

I adjust my lead-lined cboardman shorts, circle the plant and cut inland a little. I follow the Hadrian's Cycleway (HCW) signs onto some nice trails; traffic free until a fast downhill into Egremont.

A pretty little town with a wide main street and quite a well-preserved castle, especially considering Robert the Bruce attacked the town in 1322 causing a huge death toll.

Egremont Castle

I carried my bike up the steps to sit inside the ruins and have a sandwich but as I sat down Sue and Eve rang to ask where I was and told me they were in the main street below.

Carrying my laden bike back down the steps I gurned my displeasure at being summoned and thought about World Champion Gurner Peter Jackman, who had all his teeth pulled out to compete, in what is known as a real artform in Egremont.

The town is also famous for it's Crab Fair as well as greasy pole climbing and wrestling. It is claimed the fair goes back to 1267.

Sue has parked the van in the town and wants me to help guide her out as she's not that comfortable reversing yet.

A large crowd gathers as she puts the vehicle into reverse. I stand in the street waving my arms like a helicopter shouting, 'Go, go, go!'.

Eve covers her face with embarrassment as locals and tourists alike stop to stare at this idiot shouting encouragement to a campervan.

On I pedal, alternating between roads and lanes heading for Whitehaven. It's about this time that the HCW meets (or joins) the C2C route and I can't help thinking I'll be cycling the same trail in a week's time.

I wind my way along the track and enjoy a great downhill, free wheeling for a few miles. Then I encounter the 'Rhydyfelin' of the north – that part of a major cycle trail that is covered in smashed glass bottles, discarded needles and other detritus with dodgy-looking, pale youngsters lurking behind bushes.

I pass a young mother with four small children and can't help overhear the conversation.

"Mam, is that where they found the dead body?"

"Yeh I think so love..."

I increase my pace and soon I'm leaving the council estate and pedalling onto the harbour front. I see the Beacon museum, the marina and all the boats and am pleased the first day is almost done without too much hassle.

The wonder of texts means Eve is there to take a photo of me as I discover the metal C2C sign.

We meet up and decide to grab a beer in a local hostelry. Lili is excited to see me and all the locals fuss her too. We sit outside The Vine pub but they didn't seem to serve much. Eve wanted to look around 'New Look', 'Primark' or some similar shop so off she went while Sue failed to secure a coffee.

C2C sign at Whitehaven

An interesting fact about Whitehaven is that it is the site of the last invasion of England. It was during the

American War of Independence when a drunken Scottish lad set fire to a ship.

Back on the trail I cycle along the lovely seafront before heading inland and uphill. It's a nice trail, fair bit of uphill but not too hard to cycle.

It's a great trail into Workington town and I've finished for the day.

One of three theatres in Workington

I wander up and down the main shopping street then realize our campsite is inland somewhere and I've already passed it. I contemplate a quick game of 'uppies and downies' but I'm not really 'up' for it so I sit 'down', phone Sue and Eve and ask for a lift.

The campsite is a few miles out of town, off the trail,

at Gale Brow (01900 873373). It's a bargain at £17 for the van, the three of us and the dog. The showers are hot and I'm soon cracking open my first bottle of lager to toast the first day done.

We walk up the hill to Oilys pub (strange name?). I have chicken fajitas and chips plus two pints of Ennervale pale ale. Eve has a huge vegetarian concoction and Sue has scampi. The lovely food is only spoilt by the swarms of wasps around us in the beer garden. Not the pubs fault of course just that it was a good summer for wasps.

We walk back to the campsite and Eve decides she'll sleep in the front of the van which doesn't make me too happy, especially as I've just sweated my nuts off erecting my little one-man tent, blown the air bed up and put my pillow and sleeping bag inside!

I dismantle the tent to save time for tomorrow, still cursing teenagers under my breath. It's about then that I realise my bad back is alive and well.

Cycling Stats

Start: 9:30am
Distance: 30.53 miles
Total Distance: 30.53 miles
Average Speed: 10.3 mph
Fastest Speed: 25.8 mph
Cycling Time: 5 hrs 21 mins
Finish: 4:00pm
Calories: 1989
Ascent: 294m
Descent: 294m
Beers: 3

Route

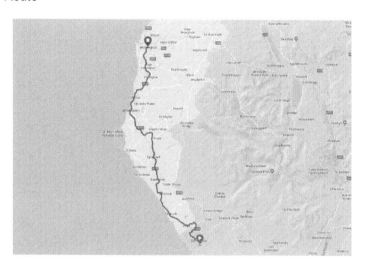

Hill Profile

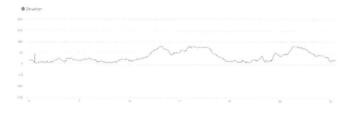

 Day 3

Workington to Brampton
Sunday 4th August 2019

iPhone alarm: Three Coins In The Fountain – Frank Sinatra

Up 6:00am, light rain – great. On the road by 7:40am and a morale boosting downhill until the cycle path ends on a busy road after less than a mile. What now?

Wind turbines just past campsite

Ah well, I trust in Buddha and turn ninety degrees left and head in the vague direction of the coast on a country lane. For once the gods on my side and I enjoy a massive stretch downhill until I reach a village T-junction. Instinct says to turn right (north ish) but for some reason I turn left (it just felt better). As it turns out it was the right decision and the road slowly bends around to face the coast.

I reach Workington (déjà vu) but then I'm completely lost as there are no signs to be found anywhere. I'm sure there are signs but that is one of the problems with town centres on Sustrans routes. Out in the country on a ten-mile straight stretch you don't really need a sign but in a town centre with a maze of streets and alleys you need lots. Maybe Sustrans can take this on board as I've found this hassle in almost every town or village I've cycled through all over the UK. Fine when you're on the route but venture one street off and you're buggered.

I ask a young girl in a sports shop and she directs me in the vague direction of the docks. I wasn't hopeful but in fairness she turns out to be right, although I went left. Lol.

Miners statue, Flimby

On the main road just north of town I ask two kind gents who were putting up posters and signs for a charity run (these guys must know the way I thought). They said the trail was half a mile back in town but I could pick it up if I continued over a bridge and headed north. This I did and soon I was back on the trail with the accompanying Roman helmet graphics on – phew!

This was a great section, parallel to the main road on a cycle trail. It was very flat, hardly any wind and I got up to a good speed. I pass the *New Balance* shoe factory before heading inland.

Stunning, deserted coastline

I'm now heading uphill on country lanes and then more downhill to the village of Flimby. Back on the coast I reach Maryport, which has a nice feel to it.

In the past the Romans and Normans built castles here and in more recent times the town had a thriving industrial base but by the 1930s the town was a ghost town with unemployment almost 60%. The future must be tourism but I found the town quite quaint anyway.

I chat to a man and his dog (the dog wasn't that helpful to be honest) who tells me he's cycled the way I'm going. He advises of a shortcut inland to miss the headland around Bowness-on-Solway. He says there's not much to see there even though I know it's a nature reserve so for me probably a lovely area.

Pedalling along the promenade, which is quiet and lovely I notice loads of offshore wind turbines, which reminds me of the north Wales coastline on my 2016 ride.

Then R72 turns in and I cycle past farms down country lanes. I stop for a drink and consult my Google Maps on the mobile.

Mmm? Something seems amiss. I seem to have fifty-five plus miles still to go yet I've done twenty odd already. I look at my printed off sheets from the tourist website that details the Hadrian's cycleway. I add up the different mileages on the sheet between towns. Mmm? Strange.

"Oh bollocks!"

Musical locals

My brain suddenly registers what the maths is telling me. I've miscalculated by assuming Google is taking me the cycle route when it says under the route (using cycle route...). It isn't.

Anyway the long and short of it is that if I head around the peninsular I'll be adding on at least twenty-five, maybe thirty miles to today's route. I told myself I'd never cycle over fifty miles in a day again so this is not on. I decide to cut cross-country and lose some miles.

I take a photo of some locals and can't help thinking about Pink Floyd again. I 'meddle' with my mobile, 'meddle' with my snacks, 'meddle' with my drinks and have now 'meddled' with my route. Get it?

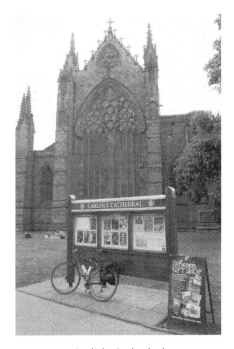

Carlisle Cathedral

My detour takes me to Abbeytown, then Wigtown and on to Micklethwaite. Eventually I leave the B roads and lanes and grab the main A road into Carlisle. It's a bit busy but I only have a few miles to go. I text Sue and Eve to see if they are nearby.

I stop at a Spar and buy a can of 'Monster' drink. The

drugs help a bit and soon I'm cycling in agony with a bad back and a sore chest into the city centre.

Seeing the castle I know I'm quite near the main shopping street so text Sue to meet me by the 'cross tower thing' in the middle of town. The gang is reunited and Lili gives me a nice fuss.

I like Carlisle and remember me and Derek had a good night here when we cycled LEJOG back in 2005. The city has one of the bloodiest histories in the UK though.

The 'Curse of Carlisle' was a 16th Century curse raised by Archbishop Dunbar of Glasgow in 1525 against the Border Reivers, who survived by stealing cattle. For the millennium celebrations, the local council commissioned a 14-tonne granite artwork inscribed with all 1,069 words of the curse. Following the installation of the stone, Carlisle suffered floods, foot-and-mouth disease, job losses and a goal famine for the football team.

I decide to have a pint, head to the Kings Head and soon strike up a conversation with a local archaeologist. I pull up a stool but the barman says, "You're not allowed to do that."

I look around at the hordes of customers on this mental Sunday, two others.

"Will people really notice?" I ask.

"Pub policy I'm afraid."

"OK, I'll just stand in the way instead."

Meanwhile my bone and artefact-loving friend takes me on a tour of the UK, telling me all the places he's drunk in and dug up bodies.

I mention that Melvyn Bragg came from Carlisle and he tells me that he didn't know that.

"Carlisle was also the place that had the first letter-box, back in 1853," I say.

"Really?"

"Yeh, and did you know that Cumbria has more

microbreweries than any other county?"

Fed up with drinking with Michael Caine my friend notes, "Wales's rugby team is really good now."

He knew how to change the subject I'll give him that.

Beer drained we say our goodbyes and good lucks and I say hello to Lili again.

Sue has found the campsite we're to stay at and says they'll head there soon. I still have a few miles to cycle so head off too.

I pedal around the city again but am soon lost. No cycle route signs! I use Google Maps again and my mobile battery is not happy. Eventually I use the subway, pass the University and am heading for Rickerby Park.

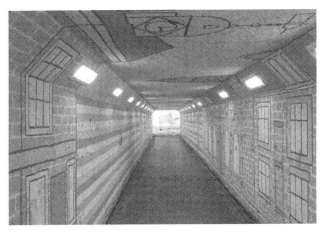

Subway

I cross the River Eden and soon I'm back in the countryside, even though I can still hear the sound of the main A road somewhere close.

Stopping to ask a girl for directions I end up doing a survey about my use of the park. It starts to rain.

Pedalling on I reach Brampton, which is quite a pretty

town. I cycle through town, turn up a short hill and down a lane before reaching our rather posh campsite at Irthing Vale (01697 389111), which sets us back £25, but at least we have a hookup that allows me to charge my devices for the next day.

After a hot shower and half an hour on the hair dryer with my soaking wet coat, shorts and shoes we decide to hit the town. I leave my clothes outside, draped over the van, to dry in the wind as it looks like quite a sunny evening now.

Arts centre, Brampton

Brampton is a lovely little place, first granted a royal Market Charter by Henry III in 1252. It also hosts the 'Brampton Live' music festival that has seen 'The Waterboys', 'Richard Thompson', 'Suzanne Vega' and many others play here.

I take a photo of the arts centre and we head for the Nags Head pub.

I took a photo of Sue and hand her the camera so she can reciprocate and snap me and Eve.

Sue in Nags Head

Unfortunately, Sue is used to a more sophisticated camera model, a professional DSLR with a 50mm prime lens, set to aperture setting where she can really go low with her f stops, blur the background and produce an almost dream-like creation that even Annie Leibovitz would be proud of. I only have the point and press waterproof Olympus with me though.

Sue found it quite difficult to operate the camera

when trying to capture me and Eve and after six or eighteen efforts (says Eve) we eventually get a shot that can grace the inside of this classy manuscript.

Still laughing we head for the Howard Arms and beer number two. Now it has to be said that most pubs we go to these days are dog friendly but this pub takes the biscuit (or should that be dog biscuit). We were greeted at the door by a very sociable black labradoodle-type mutt, then upon entry had three or four other pups to negotiate our way past before we made it to the bar. Then we watched as yet more dogs of all shapes and sizes sat around the tables, waiting for food to drop from the customers dining there. We headed up the stairs and into the quieter back room. Yep, a family with a dog. I looked outside in the beer garden – more dogs! Honestly, this was doggie heaven. Lili loved it.

Various attempts by Sue to press shutter at the 'precise moment'

Then the heavens opened and it tipped down with rain. In fact it was 'hoyin it doown'. My clothes are soaked again. We order a Chinese and take it back to the campsite where we discover that the good people of Cumbria don't half like big portions, and I can eat!

Meal over, stomach aching I decide to resort to hair dryer duty again on my cycling shorts. Ah the joys of camping.

Cycling Stats

Start: 7:40am
Distance: 57.84 miles
Total Distance: 88.37 miles
Average Speed: 11.4 mph
Fastest Speed: 32.6 mph
Cycling Time: 8 hrs 36 mins
Finish: 5:30pm
Calories: 3623
Ascent: 287m
Descent: 340m
Beers: 3

Route

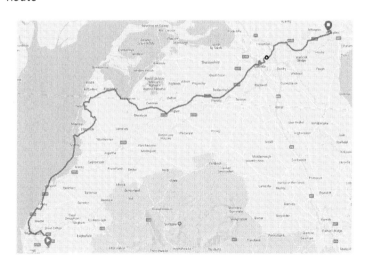

Hill Profile

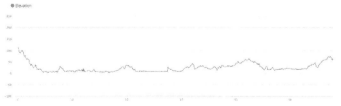

Day 4

Brampton to Wylam
Monday 5th August 2019

iPhone alarm: Here Come The Romans – Cherry Ghost

"Right! Today's the day," I shout through a hoarse throat.

"I'm tired," replies Eve.

Start of touristy bit

"I think you've got my cold," says Sue, as she watches and listens to a thick green dawn chorus best left unmentioned.

Up by 6:00am, quick wash and breakie of beans and egg. Then I return to the hair dryer until I'm happy my clothes are reasonably dry.

Today was the day too. Eve had changed her mind about being bored for two days and thankfully abandoned the idea of going back to Carlisle to catch a bus to Cardiff. We would see the wall today I had told her.

I'm on the road by 8:40am and minutes after I leave the town I head up a country lane to the start of the Hadrian's Wall Tourist Trail. I stop to take a selfie.

A few ups and downs before a nice downhill, across the River Irthing and I'm in Lanercost, where the priory is situated.

Lanercost Priory

The beautiful setting of Augustinian Lanercost Priory is close to the famous wall and as such it suffered frequent attacks during the long Anglo-Scottish wars, once by Robert the Bruce himself.

Like many of the historic sites in this part of the world it is English Heritage that is responsible for their upkeep. As a result they charge entry fees for most sites. Unfortunately for me I hadn't factored in this cost and so gave most a miss, even though some are only £5 or so. A good idea might be to buy a card for the year that entitles you to free entry to all sites. Good value if you're going to visit a few of the attractions.

First sight of the famous wall

Cycling on I encounter a mother of a hill towards Banks. I cycle a fair bit of the hill but when the Sustrans route takes me on a detour to yet more uphill I get a bit fed up so stop and push for a bit. What is the point exactly? Fine if you're a masochist like my friend Derek, or Geraint Thomas, but a winding country lane is only good if it avoids the traffic, shortens the trail or provides some additional beauty or site to see.

I jump back in the saddle as it's early in the day and as I reach the top I'm rewarded with my first site of the famous wall.

The 'Banks East' section of the wall is the best-preserved turret or observation tower in the western sector of Hadrian's Wall.

Originally there were two turrets to every Roman mile along the length of Hadrian's Wall, each manned by a few soldiers watching over the frontier to the north. Banks East Turret remained in use until late in the 4th Century.

Long, intact section next to a straight road

As I take a few photos I notice some German tourists climbing all over the wall.

"Oi, that wall is nearly two thousand years old, but it

won't last another two thousand if you keep crawling over it with you're great big jackboots!"

I get a funny look but I think I've got away with it.

Pedalling on again and being careful to avoid a speeding Saxon people carrier I find more bits of old wall, although in fairness I think other people found it before me.

I reach Birdoswald and get a text from Eve. They've driven up to Gretna Green and Eve has added another country to her ever-growing list.

An hour or so later I get another message telling me that her and Sue are taking Lili for a walk behind the priory so they aren't far behind now.

A Roman soldier waiting for his KFC

The fort here was occupied by Romans from 112 AD to 400 AD and the wall was originally built from turf. Another thing the Romans brought to our shores was the concept of fast food and street stalls. At Birdoswald, where many soldiers were based, having access to tasty 'food-on-the-go' was essential. The Romans also introduced apples, pears and peas to the UK.

The wall has a two-mile section at this point and when Eve and Sue arrive they walk Lili alongside the wall for a bit so she doesn't miss out either.

Immediately after the fort is a big downhill, followed by an equally nasty uphill and soon I leave Cumbria and enter Northumberland at Gilsland.

A nice downhill is followed by, yes you guessed it, a massive uphill. A truly horrible 14% section. I pushed the bike up and admired the storm clouds racing away a few miles north of me.

Rewarded with an awesome downhill into Haltwhistle I realise I've only clocked fourteen miles so far, with twenty-three to go to Hexham.

Hadrian's Cycleway signpost

I pause at Haltwhistle, hoping to have some luck like the workmen in 1836 who found a copper pot with sixty-three Roman coins in it when quarrying one day. Although some tribes in southern England produced coins before the Romans arrived it was their coinage that was used as proper currency to buy things. A denarius minted in Rome could be spent in Britain, North Africa or Turkey. A global currency on this scale has not been seen since!

I pedal on, up hill and down hill. I reach Bardon Mill and Vindolanda, then Haydon Bridge before finally Hexham where I indulge in a Coop 'meal deal' of prawn salad, veggie pastie and kiwi / lime juice smoothie.

Pushing up the hill into town I sit below the clock and stare at the gaol while I ingest calories to top up my wasting frame (yeh really) ☺

Being a border town the place has seen a few skirmishes over the years. William Wallace burnt the town in 1297 and crafty Robert the Bruce threatened the same fate in 1312 but settled for £2,000 protection money instead.

The old gaol, one of Britain's first

Hexham Abbey was originally a monastery but with stones taken from Corbridge or Hadarian's Wall it was reinforced. Vandals!

I cross the River Tyne and although I've probably criss-crossed it quite a bit already today it's the first time I realise it. It's my first real glimpse of the famous waterway and I'm surprised at how big, wide and fast flowing it is. Then I'm back on R76 and heading for Corbridge through country lanes.

Stopping off to take a photo of the lovely ruins I don't pay the £7.90 entrance fee to go inside. Unlike many fortified sections of the wall Corbridge was once a bustling town and supply base where Romans and locals could pick up food and supplies. It stayed a lively community until the end of Roman Britain in the early years of the 5th Century.

Hexham Abbey

I cycle on and enter the modern town proper. It's very 'Cotswoldie' town (if there is such a word) and I see a sign for Watling Street, which makes me feel I'm really in Roman Britain.

Having said that there are quite a few 'Watling Street's in the UK, the main one down south running for 200 miles from Canterbury across to Shropshire. The Romans continued this original Briton track and extended it way up north past Hadrian's Wall.

As all Monty Python fans know the Romans did many wonderful things for us, and straight roads were just one of them. Building reliable transport routes was a necessity of such an expansive empire, so having proper roads was in the Romans interest more than ours but it's still nice to see signs of their legacy still functioning.

Corbridge ruins

The town of Corbridge is full of buses and old people when I arrive so I assume it's on the tourist trail. It's a lovely looking place though and I'm severely tempted to sample a local ale in The Angel as the sun shines and I strip off a layer to enjoy some real August weather again.

I have such a strong sense of duty that I pass up the chance of a beer and then regret a mile later.

I'm enjoying the rolling countryside, the beautiful

yellow fields bright in the summer sun when a sneaky little 13% creeps up on me. It's a short hill though so I manage alright. I'm three miles from Wylam so maybe I should have had that beer, especially as it isn't that far to the end of the day's cycling.

A nice downhill, over Ovingham Bridge and I'm cycling along the river again but now on the south side. I cycle on trails for a bit before crossing back over the iron railway bridge at Wylam. I'm back on the north bank of the River Tyne again. I follow more lovely trails and can feel the town isn't far now.

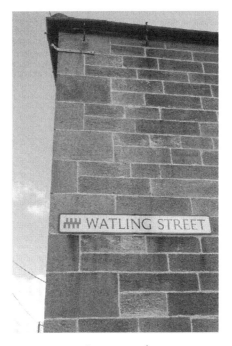

Roman road

I'm getting a second wind now and whizzing along the flat trail when I suddenly feel the need to stop myself and check where I am. For once my iPhone seems to still have some charge left on it so I consult good ole 'evil' Google.

Yep, my sixth sense has worked again. I'm actually at Wylam, on the trail just under the Fox and Hounds pub.

The Angel, Corbridge

I'm feeling a bit knackered all of a sudden but phone Sue to ask where they are and discover they arrived about five minutes ago. Sue meets me outside the Black Bull Inn, where we've booked in to have a proper rest and clean up, although they don't do breakfast, which is a shame.

There is no car park but the campervan is parked across the road in a side street so we head there to sort out my kit and put the bike inside the van.

After a shower and a quick change we walk around town but soon realise that Wylam is kind of shut on a Monday, especially as regards anyone cooking us a hearty meal. None of the pubs did food, apart from the extortionate 'The Ship Inn'.

The barman in the Fox and Hounds directs us to the pizza place – 'The Wood Oven', which looks like it's in someone's front room. Alas, the pizza place is shut. This would never do in Roman times.

Wylam Railway Bridge

I have a pint of Stella to wash my sinuses out and chat to a few locals, one of whom is home from Australia and is going out with a girl from near Wrexham. His friend offers to take us on a tour of the town and directs us to the 'chinkie' at the top of the hill. Such a gentleman!

My head cold and tight chest are really taking their toll now and I'm sweating like Josef Fritzl on 'Grand Designs'. I'm burning up big time so decide to make paracetamol my friend for the next few days.

The Chinese meal is huge again and we can't eat it all. Even Lili struggles with the leftovers.

Cycling Stats

Start: 8:40am
Distance: 47.15 miles
Total Distance: 135.52 miles
Average Speed: 10.9 mph
Fastest Speed: 33.4 mph
Cycling Time: 7 hrs 51 mins
Finish: 5:30pm
Calories: 3427
Ascent: 562m
Descent: 603m
Beers: 1

Route

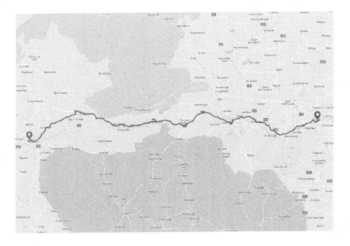

Hill profile

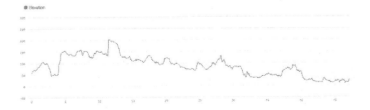

 # Day 5

Wylam to Washington
Tuesday 6th August 2019

iPhone alarm: A Big Day In The North – Black Grape

The mattress is the softest in the world, which might sound nice but when you're constantly rolling into the middle of the bed it's a pain. Not that I had that problem for long though as by about 3:00am Lili the labradoodle decides she wants to join in the fun too and jumps up onto the bed pushing me to the edge and once again my back is in pieces by the time I attempt to move in the morning.

Black Bull Inn

Breakie sandwich of salmon and egg, which Sue bought in the Coop last night, is delicious and I wash it down with a nice cup of tea. Sue rubs some Tesco's own 'deep heat' in my back and I rub some Ibuprofen gel into my knees and wrist. Yep, I'm falling apart.

It's much cooler today and I add a layer as I rejoin the cycle route exactly where I left it yesterday. Within half a mile I stop at George Stephenson's house but it's closed.

His 'Locomotive 1' was the first steam engine to carry passengers on a public line, the Stockton and Darlington Railway in 1825 although Cornishman Richard Trevithick used a steam engine to haul a train from Merthyr to Abercynon in 1804.

George Stephenson's house

I have no idea where I'll finish tonight but know I must try to add a few more miles to the journey if possible. I was really looking forward to this morning but by 0.9 miles I realise the stabbing pain in my knees might not be agreeing with me. Plus my back is about to go into spasm and my spokes are twanging.

Ever the boy scout I rub more anti-inflammatory gel into my human parts and use a spoke key on the front wheel.

Maybe I should have done this the other way around.

Five miles later my wheel seems OK but my back isn't. I'm cycling with one hand on the handlebars and one permanently massaging my lower back as I enjoy the site of the great river again.

Soon I see bridges upon bridges as I approach Newcastle quayside – one of the highlights of the trip.

Bridges

Newcastle is on the northern bank of the River Tyne and is about nine miles from the North Sea. The city was actually founded by Emperor Hadrian in the 2nd Century AD and parts of the wall can still be seen along the West Road.

William the Conqueror's eldest son, Robert Curthose, built a castle here in 1080 and the city took its name from that. Important in the wool trade as the city grew it became synonymous with shipbuilding and became one of the largest shipbuilding centres in the world by the 20th Century.

There was a corruption scandal over the development of the city in the 1960s, which was alluded to in the excellent TV series 'Our Friends In The North', which is well worth a watch if you haven't seen it.

I paused under the Tyne Bridge, sent a text to Sue to tell her that there was a Wetherspoons here and a car park if they wanted to have a look around the city.

My back had settled down a little by now although I was in need of some glucose. Ironically, Lucozade was first made in Newcastle in 1927 by Thomas Beech.

I'd been to this awesome city a few times before and wanted to stay but knew I had more miles to do. I pushed my bike under the bridge where a sign reminds you of the Great North Run, a half marathon that attracts 57,000 runners every year. I also couldn't help notice all the seagulls nesting under the bridge. On closer inspection I could tell they were kittiwakes.

Grade II listed Swing Bridge, site of the original Roman 'Pons Aelius'

The River Tyne has supported the most inland breeding colony of kittiwakes in the world since 1960. Each spring, these pelagic gulls return to the Newcastle-Gateshead Quayside where they nest on buildings and other structures, including the Tyne Bridge. The kittiwakes are now part of this iconic cityscape and a tourist attraction in their own right.

As I passed underneath (avoiding the whiter areas of the cycle path for obvious reasons) I looked up to see hundreds of Kittiwakes had already nested here this breeding season. Not all residents want the birds here but as an important 'red species' whose numbers have declined drastically due to climate change and over fishing I think it's the least we can do to allow them to stay. They are a cute sea bird and have a really cool name too.

Kittiwakes nesting under the Tyne Bridge

I decided to walk across the Millennium Bridge so I could look back and take a photo of the iconic Tyne Bridge. The bridge was designed by Mott, Hay and Anderson who also designed the Sydney Harbour Bridge. The original design was derived from the Hell Gate Bridge in New York though.

There is too much to say about Newcastle but worth a mention for history buffs is the famous dialect. And something the stuffy BBC should take more heed of. The 'Geordie' vocabulary, with its distinctive words, has its origins in the original Anglo-Saxon that the peoples who moved into the north after the Romans left spoke.

The English spoken in the rest of the country seems to have been influenced more by Latin and Norman while in Newcastle the language is still more pure although Scandinavian words have also found their way in.

Plaque

Half of me wanted to have a conversation with a local but most people (apart from the homeless sleeping under the kittiwakes) were busy moving too fast (as is often the case in thriving city centres) but the other half of me was glad as I probably wouldn't have understood a word of it. Unless I happened upon Mr Bean of course. (Rowan Atkinson, although from Consett went to Newcastle University).

Another important cultural aspect of the city to

mention is the music. 'The Animals', 'Sting' (of 'The Police' and not doing sex properly fame) as well as awesome guitarist and songwriter Mark Knopfler of 'Dire Straits' all hail from the city or nearby. Actually 'Sting' comes from Wallsend which is where Hadarian's 'wall' 'ends'.

Iconic view, Newcastle

Other artistic connections with the city are Lindisfarne, Brian Johnson (AC/DC) and Jimmy Nail of 'Auf Wiedersehen, Pet' fame.

I'm glad there is no 'fog on the Tyne' and pedal on. My back is still sore but luckily my chest infection is taking my mind off it as I return to the cycle path and say goodbye to the city.

I stop to take a photo of a great-looking pub as I leave the city and head for Tynemouth.

The wind is picking up now and I see a large sign for the HCW, which is reassuring. At least I'm heading the right way.

The trail is lovely all the way to Tynemouth although it's quite sad to see some of the run-down areas around the docks that are now closed or stagnating since the heavy industry got closed down during Thatcher's era.

The Tyne pub

Hadrian's Cycleway arch

I also can't help notice some awesome looking old pubs, mostly closed but with stories to tell no doubt. Such a shame that much of the heritage of a country has been lost, the characters too.

Tynemouth

Giant route artwork

Pedalling for about nine or ten miles I eventually

reach the coast and take my time to look around. It's a weird place but I like it. Somewhat run-down but you get the impression that it might be a nice place to live.

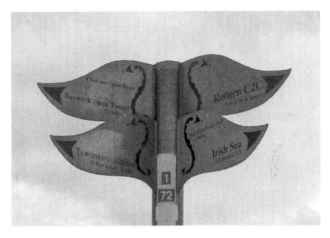

C2C sign

There are signs that new developments are planned and that this will soon be a new yuppie town for ponytail-clad, girly bike pushing, new media types with beards and lumberjack shirts who like to talk about organic fairtrade coffee and craft ale. Or maybe I'm just a sad and bitter old man? Time will tell.

Taking photos I notice it starts to feel a little chilly. I push on to the end of the route, get to the signpost (although one is missing), then walk around and look across to the castle and priory.

Then it starts to rain. Then it suddenly turns stormy and so I quickly abandon my sightseeing and go back down the hill, along the front and shelter in a 'Gents' toilets. (That's my excuse anyway).

Then I notice the lack of mirrors. Is this a northern thing I ask myself? Pubs, campsites – none of them have had mirrors! Perhaps 'Geordie' folk are just not that vain? Maybe there is a glass shortage here?

Trying to be arty – 'Lighthouse through benches'

The rain is obviously in for the day so I decide to cut my losses and head back out of town a mile or so and try to find the ferry.

It would have been nice to have stopped for some fish and chips, which I got the impression was going to be about as fresh as one could get what with all the fishing boats nearby but alas I'm running out of time.

I pass the 'Prince of Wales' pub and the wooden dolly. The original figurehead was erected by shipowner Alexander Bartleman in 1814. It was customary for sailors to cut off small chunks to bring them luck but this ritual eventually destroyed the poor dolly.

In 1850, the dolly was attacked by a group of drunken vandals who broke her neck and ripped her body from the ground. She has been replaced by a number of new dollies, each of which has suffered a similar fate. Must be a local game?

Ferry to South Shields

Before we leave I must briefly mention one of Tynemouth's most famous sons. Stan Laurel (Rob Howley's dad) who although being born in Cumbria lived here between the ages of seven and eleven and loved the place.

I easily find my way to the passenger ferry terminal (smaller than some bus terminals actually) and wait in the pouring down rain for the boat.

Enduring twenty minutes of raspberry-blowing kids in the heavy rain before the ferry arrives seems like some kind of test but I'm soon cheered up and pleasantly surprised when I discover how cheap it is. Just £1.70 for a single – bargain!

Ten minutes or so later we're embarking in South Shields, where 'Alien', 'Blade Runner' and 'Thelma and Louise' director Ridley Scott is from.

There is a short respite in the rain and I leave the ferry and cycle to the official end of the route, about a mile out is the Arbeia Roman Fort and a helpful sign that declares you have reached the end of the Hadarian's Cycleway.

Arbeia Roman fort

It's a nice feeling although a shame I have no-one to share it with.

End of the Hadrian's Cycleway

I stop for a drink and a chewy bar, take some photos but then notice a primary school opposite. Soon a load of children are heading for the fort and I decide it best I vacate the area before someone shouts 'paedo' or something as they see a strange man in lycra loitering outside the gates of the fort, staring at kids through the railings.

It's nice that I've finished my first planned ride but I'm now completely lost as nowhere does it say where the C2C route might be? There is no handy, helpful arrow pointing towards the west coast so I eventually decide that being lost is good. Not a bit lost of course, that is no good, but completely lost. Yeh, completely lost is great because anyway is right.

Sea to Sea (C2C)

The C2C is officially the 'Sea to Sea' but most people say the 'Coast to Coast' when referring to the route that is best ridden from west to east to take advantage of the south-westerly prevailing winds. Also the gradients are supposed to be kinder this way round, with longer downhill sections and shorter uphills. Trust me to be facing the wrong way eh!

Apparently it's the UK's most popular challenge cycle route, which doesn't surprise me as it's a great trail through varied countryside and isn't too long either.

As I was doing it in reverse, after I left the coast I would be ascending the railway paths of County Durham, climbing over the Pennines (known as 'the roof of England'), visiting old mining towns, before passing through the northern Lake District to reach the coast and hopefully return to Whitehaven, which I'd passed through on my first day.

Many riders follow the tradition of dipping their back wheel in the Irish Sea at the start of the journey and their front wheel in the North Sea when they finish. I couldn't find a way down to the sea in Tynemouth so missed christening the bike in the North Sea but was determined I'd put my front tyre in at Whitehaven.

Sustrans and partners opened the route in 1994 and it includes Black Hill, the highest point on the National Cycle Network (609m) and the Consett-Sunderland railway path and sculpture trail.

The route uses R14, R7 and R71.

*

I decide to use R1 to Sunderland and go from there, which is lucky because a few miles later Sue texts me to say she's found a hotel in Washington. (Note to future self – write it down).

Consulting the map I can see that that will do nicely and so I head for the seaside city of Sunderland, threading my way through houses on and off cycle trails.

The rain is well and truly hammering down now as I pass Souter Lighthouse, which is famous for being the first lighthouse in the world to be actually designed and built specifically to use AC current. First lit in the 1870s, Souter was described at the time as 'without doubt one of the most powerful lights in the world'.

Souther lighthouse

It's heavy showers now and I cycle quickly between bus stops to shelter as I head south on a lovely seaside cycle trail. I eat a chewy bar to keep my energy levels up but could really do with a hot bowl of soup of the day.

A nice downhill takes me past Seaburn, a lovely sandy beach that reminds me of Barry Island with your typical, tacky seaside arcades. I stop to take a photo of the picturesque Roker Pier then shelter again where I strike up a conversation with two local lady cyclists who inform me that this is the posh part of the city and there are rougher bits best avoided.

Roker Pier

The ladies also explain to me about the county boundaries that have been confusing me. Northumberland is one, Durham is another but both Newcastle and Sunderland are in Tyne and Wear.

Windmill

This makes sense, especially when you look at the map and the two river estuaries.

Thinking about a lack of mirrors earlier, it's ironic how I now pass The National Glass Centre, which is located in Sunderland, on the north banks of the River Wear. I stop for a quick photo of the only C2C sign I can find, near the University, and go for the 'unlit' route along the docks rather than inland and past the 'City of Light' football stadium. Always been a rugby fan so no huge loss to miss it.

C2C sign, near University

Then it really empties down, like a power shower. I attempt to shelter under some trees but it is raining so heavy that this proves to be pointless and before long I'm soaked to the skin.

Sunderland grew up as a port, trading in coal and salt before becoming a shipbuilding centre like Newcastle. Following the decline in the industry though it now focuses on cars, science and the service sector.

It's a shame the weather is so bad as the cycle trail is excellent and I wish I had more time to explore. There seems to be lots of interesting sights in Sunderland that will have to wait for another time.

Docks, Sunderland

Giving up sheltering from the rain I push on and keeping on the C2C route I'm soon not that far from Washington. Fab, I think to myself, hot shower here I come...

The trails are great although a bit rough and better suited to a mountain bike perhaps. There's loads of muddy puddles, which give me a colonic irrigation, but I'm nearly home so carry on. My sixth sense kicks in again as I seem to be at Washington already so I stop to look for a town centre but there doesn't appear to be one.

I can't help thinking about chef from 'Apocalypse Now' – *'Don't get off the trail. Not unless you were going all the way.'*

I check my crappy iPhone 5 that was 100% charged this morning and I've only used 'Notes' and the odd bit of Google Maps and then it dies.

"F***** h***," I scream, "I hate Apple."

As I curse my dependency on technology I wonder what we ever did before phones?

OK, calm down Dave, no problem. Right, what was the address of the place Sue booked for us to stay?

I can't remember. It was in a text.

Don't panic I tell myself. Just find the centre of town. There's probably a clock tower and a market place or something. Mmm. Yeh, do that and ask someone I reassure myself.

I cycle about four or five miles around in circles past various roundabouts, housing estates and main roads until I happen upon a young lad in the car park of a plastic pub.

"How laddie, yee lost?"

"Yeh, I am." I explain my predicament.

His mate turns up as he tries to warn me about a spider that's crawling down the inside of my coat.

"What yee on aboot gadgie?"

"Ahm just telling yee like."

"What the f***, he doesn't want te knaa aboot tha."

"Well ah divvent knaa."

His mate is trying to hide his amusement now.

"Well gadgie what if ah divvent tell the guy an he cycles off then sees this spider leik?"

I decide these lads might not be much help.

"Divvent yee knaa yer missus number then?"

"No idea of numbers buttie."

Now I have to admit I start to panic a bit but eventually get directions from a number of people (a young lass, a bloke at a bus stop and a dog walker) to a place called 'the galleries' and find a leisure centre. I explain the situation and the very kind lady and lovely young lad on reception allow me to ring my Mam, back in Wales. (The only number I can remember).

Not the best with phones I ask for Sue's mobile number.

"Hi Mam, can you do me a favour, I need to get hold of Sue but…"

My mam puts the phone down and rings Sue.

I ring back. Engaged. Eventually…

"Mam, don't hang up. Listen."

"Yes. Everything alright? How is the dog? How is Eve? Is she eating? I went to town today, is it raining there, they say there is a hurricane coming your way, be careful on that bike…"

"Mam. My phone is out of battery. Can you ring Sue and ask her where we are staying tonight? Or tell me her mobile number?"

"Oh, OK, where is it?"

"Her number will be on your mobile mam."

"OK, hang on."

My mam finds her mobile and I wait for what seems like hours for it to turn itself on. I hear the startup sound then my mother tapping away at random buttons.

"I can't find it. How do I find it?"

"OK, doesn't matter, just ring Sue."

"Hang on."

"Hi Sue, David is on the phone, here speak to him."

I have no idea what happened next but can picture my mother holding two phones and wondering why no-one was saying anything.

"Mam. Mam. Mam."

"She can't hear you."

"OK, listen, just tell Sue I'm at the leisure centre."

"She's gone?"

"What?"

"I put the phone down on Sue. Oh, I'm confused now."

"OK, don't worry. Just ring Sue back and tell her 'Washington Leisure Centre'. Have you got that alright?"

"Washing machine leather censor. OK."

The phone goes dead.

Ah well, I'm sleeping on the floor of a leisure centre tonight I think to myself.

Waiting outside I'm starting to get cold now and my chest is tight as hell but in twenty minutes I see the welcome sign of a silver VW campervan turn into the centre and my spirits are lifted like John Wayne when he sees the cavalry approach. Good ole mam!

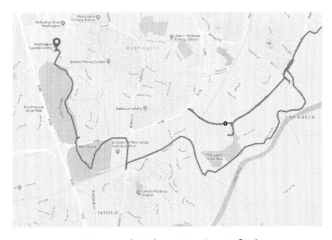

My convoluted route trying to find

the centre of Washington

Sue picks me up and we drive to the Hotel Campanile which at £44 for the three of us, and Lili, seems a bargain after the rip-off £60 for last night's digs.

I have a soak in the bath and a beer (at the same time) and get my kit draped over radiators and wash the mud from my water bottles ready for tomorrow. Don't you just love the British summer?

I take Lili for a walk around the block but am careful not to lose sight of this building such is my paranoia now. Me and Sue have fish and chips in the restaurant and I guzzle a pint of Stella but my chest and cough is really bad now so we retire to the room with a pizza and chips for Eve.

Trying to speak I realise I can't. My sore throat is worse than I thought it was and I've lost my voice. No-one is complaining.

I start to sweat like a pineapple at customs and am soon fast asleep.

Now I always try not to be too negative when talking about a place I've visited or cycled through (maybe I caught them on a bad day eh?) but I have to say that Washington wasn't my favourite place.

George Washington the first American president's family were from here but to be honest I didn't really care. Then 'out of the blue' I also remember that posh rocker, Nazi building fan and foxhunting supporter Bryan Ferry also comes from around these parts. Enough said.

Cycling Stats

Start: 8:25am
Distance: 45.28 miles
Total Distance: 180.8 miles
Average Speed: 9.2 mph
Fastest Speed: 22.1 mph
Cycling Time: 8 hrs 40 mins
Finish: 6:00pm
Calories: 2980
Ascent: 334m
Descent: 304m
Beers: 1

Route

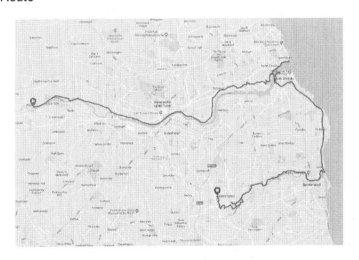

Hill profile

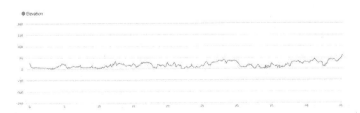

 Day 6

Washington to Nenthead
Wednesday 7th August 2019

iPhone alarm: Back In The Saddle – Aerosmith

OK, I'm ready for this. No, 'new town' nonsense was going to stop me from finding the C2C signposts, getting back on the route and whizzing out of town towards the challenge of the Pennines.

Amazing how wrong you can be. Last night I had done the boy scouts thing and screenshot two different versions of Google Maps directions from the hotel to the trail, how hard could it be to find?

Trying to find the C2C trail

Within a few hundred yards I was lost. Nothing made sense. I asked two skinheads with faces tattooed if they knew where the C2C was.

"Hi lads, any idea where the cycle trail is?"

"Weor are yee gannin?"

"Well, I was hoping Penrith but doubt I'll make it that far now, anywhere west really. Consett?"

"Are yee f****** mad mate?"

They didn't look much like Ferdinand Magellan so not a great choice on my part and they probably didn't intend to send me the wrong way but...

Then I saw two sensible-looking elderly ladies.

"Excuse me, do you know where the coast to coast cycling trail is please?"

"Yes love," they said in unison, smiling.

"Oh great!"

"You're nowhere near it."

"Oh."

They directed me to a roundabout, then told me it was behind Macro. No more than half a mile they said. A mile or two later I was near to tears. Eventually I got my useless iPhone out and used loads of data and battery power trying to find the route. I was down to 74% and I hadn't even started the ride proper!

Eventually I saw the route (by accident) below me as I crossed a bridge. I climbed down the verge with my bike and panniers under my arm. I wasn't letting it get away this time!

So pleased to finally be back on track (literally) I ignored the uphills followed by more uphills. At least they were gradual.

It's then I start to notice the beautiful County Durham countryside I'm cycling through and also notice some of the cool statues along the route.

One such piece is 'Terris Novalis' by Tony Cragg. There are two huge sculptures based on 19th Century surveyors' instruments. The theodolite stands on three stands; a human hand, a horse hoof, and the foot of a lizard type creature. The animal feet represent the symbolic heraldry found on shields, coats of arms, plaques and items associated with land ownership.

'Terris Novalis' by Tony Cragg

'Old King Coal' by David Kemp

'Terris Novalis' marks what was once Europe's largest steel works. Local people see this landmark as a monument to the scale of local industry and its demise.

'Old King Coal', which was built by volunteers and redundant miners and steelworkers is another piece of impressive artwork. Sustrans commissioned artist David Kemp to build various landmark sculptures such as this using discarded material from post-industrial sites.

Colourful legacy

I cycled on through a nice wooded area, past some metal cows (yep, very Milton *bloody* Keynes) and ignored the Beamish museum, near the town of Stanley, which aims to preserve an example of everyday life in North East England in the early 20th Century.

Then the ride got harder. It also got cold. Yep, it's still August. Then I noticed the headwind getting stronger. Some serious psychological torture was about to begin.

I see a sign for Whitehaven that says 109 miles. "Hey ho," I say, "two days." Then realise it'll take me four at this pace!

Now I'm not really a spiritual person, I'm more of a scientist but for some reason a strange shadow fell over me at this point. I suddenly became very depressed and felt really low. Probably lack of glucose. The feeling only lasted a few miles however because as I cruised through this pretty forested section what should I see standing in the middle of the track as I approached but a handsome male roe deer. I shit you not!

The original 'Bambi' was a roe deer but right wing Walt decided to make him more American for his film audience and changed him to a mule deer.

Into the Pennines

My spirits raised, onwards I pedalled but unfortunately, although I was out of the woods, I was now on the exposed moors. I thought I saw a hobby but with my eyes it was probably a kestrel.

Now my problems began in earnest as I glanced at my Garmin bike computer. I was struggling to do five mph in this strong wind. I got off for a bit and pushed. I was doing three and a half mph.

Once again I had encountered the cyclists worst nightmare, no, not a big nasty lorry – a headwind. So for the next few miles I was given a real mental test as I slogged my way along the Waskerley Way, past the reservoirs, until I eventually reached the Parkhead Station café at the top of the climb. About 1,500 feet above sea level it is a welcome break and I tucked in heartily to beans on toast for £3.50 and washed it down with a nice pot of hot tea.

Suitably replenished I re-join the rough, gravelly cycle route but then see the lovely, winding main road to my immediate right.

Great tracks, stunning open moors

"Aye why not," I say to myself. On the B6278 road I notice a sign – 17%. "Yes, at last!"

I'm soon dropping at an alarming rate and as my speed starts to rise above thirty mph I notice a few wobbles and start hearing a few telltale 'spoke' noises. The cross wind doesn't help so I touch the brakes a bit to reduce my speed down this awesome downhill.

At the bottom of the hill I join the road and forget about the trail for a bit. I need to make up some miles but I'm never going to reach Penrith so text Sue to tell her I'm aiming for Alston. She replies that she'll look for a campsite near there.

I check my maps and realise that I'm now in quite a touristy part of County Durham. I decide to stay on the road and see what turns up rather than head for Allenshead, which was the original plan.

Killhope Lead Mining Museum

The A689 road is quite quiet and a great ride. The constant headwind isn't going anywhere though and I curse my way along the banks of the River Wear. My average speed is right down as I struggle up each small hill and hardly notice the down sections.

Seeing an ominous storm cloud up ahead I pull off the road to visit the Killhope Lead Mining Museum and inject some much needed sugar into the system via a bottle of Fanta.

I leave the café and cycle across a ford to get back on the main road. I'm averaging about four or five mph now and with less than a mile to the top of the hill I take a rest to psyche myself up for the huge climb ahead.

I stop to take a photo before cycling on for a few hundred yards. Then I stop again to look for a chewy bar. This final push is going to need some calories I think to myself.

The long and winding road

Just then a fabulous customised Land Rover Discovery pulls over and John jumps out.

"Bike problems?" he asks.

"Oh no, I'm fine, just taking a rest."

"Oh, OK, going far?" he asks.

"No, not far now, but I wouldn't mind a lift to the top of that hill," I say with a wink.

John has a mountain bike strapped to the back of his beast and agrees to give me a ride. He straps the Dawes to the back and in I jump. It's only half a mile, maybe less but whilst many will see this as cheating, do you know what? I couldn't give a monkeys!

He drops me off at the top and I take a photo of the 'Welcome to Cumbria' sign. I savour the views for a minute before I'm off again. It's a fab downhill and beautiful countryside surrounds me stretching as far as the eye can see.

Huge downhill ahead!

I zoom into Nenthead and pop into the Miners Arms for a pint of Amstel lager. Only £3.50.

Nenthead's claim to fame is that it is England's highest village at 1,500 feet. It used to be a prosperous lead and silver mining centre but now relies mainly on tourists.

At the bar I chat to a nice lad called Greg. He is an

animal welfare activist and so we get on fine. He even promises to look me up on Google as for once I don't have a business card with all my books on to hand out. I warn him I'm not the Tesco CEO and off I cycle again.

A small uphill is followed by a great downhill again and I'm soon pulling over into the Haggs Bank Bunkhouse and Campsite where I see the silver VW parked up next to this really cool, blue Landie.

"Hi John," I shout.

"Bloody hell, you know someone everywhere," says Sue, amazed.

Me and John chat for a few minutes.

I wait a bit before I tell her.

Forecast not looking good

Sue cooks French toast with scrambled eggs and beans in the van while I drink a litre of Stella, as happy as a warthog in elephant dung. I have a shower in the bunkhouse and we walk Lili down by the river. It's a great campsite in a beautiful area and the owners are also really nice, as are all the people we've met up north.

After tea we look at the weather warnings again and see the forecast for Friday is pretty bad. Not hurricanes but some serious storms, thunder and lightning, heavy rain and high winds in the morning. Basically far too dangerous to be cycling in. The decision is sort of made for me. Thursday will be cloudy but dry. The calm before the low pressure front comes in overnight. I don't want to do it but have no choice really as my days of cycling seventy miles are over I reckon.

We reluctantly decide that tomorrow Sue will drive me and the bike about twenty miles further down the road to Penrith and I'll start from there. I should be able to cycle the rest of the way, through the lakes to the coast and finish in Whitehaven, just a bit further north from where I started a week ago.

It'll mean we cut our holiday a day short but we won't be able to do or see much in the rain so it's just as well.

Cycling Stats

Start: 8:25am
Distance: 46.01 miles
Total Distance: 226.81 miles
Average Speed: 8.7 mph
Fastest Speed: 34.0 mph
Cycling Time: 8 hrs 33 mins
Finish: 6:30pm
Calories: 3387
Ascent: 1009m
Descent: 699m
Beers: 1

Route

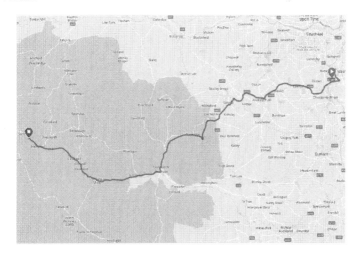

Hill Profile

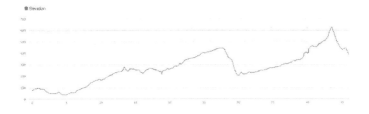

# Day 7

Penrith to Whitehaven
Thursday 8th August 2019

iPhone alarm: Should I Stay Or Should I Go – The Clash

I wake up and my back is in two. Sue rubs some Ibuprofen gel in and gives me a massage but I can still hardly walk.

Lili at Haggs Bank

Eventually I make it out of the campervan and take

Lili for a short walk down to the river below the campsite. It's a lovely morning, fresh and misty.

We drive to Alston, I miss out on some massive downhills, which is such a shame, before we stop at Penrith.

The name Penrith is very Welsh in nature (pen – head, rhydd – ford) although the river Eamont is about a mile away.

Ruins of Penrith Castle

Sue parks the campervan in town and I struggle onto the bike for my last day in the seat. I stop to snap the ruins of Penrith Castle as I leave town. Built between 1399 and 1470 as a defence against the raiding Scots.

I take the A66 as the C2C route is not obvious although it could be my addiction to painkillers that is causing the confusion. Soon I see an off road sign though and spend the next hour or so alternating between some trails, country lanes and the main road. Some of the C2C runs alongside the A road which is great 'cos you know you're not being taken miles off course.

I'm now in the 'lakes' proper. Established in 1951 the

Lake District is the largest National Park in England, which attracts over sixteen million visitors each year. The only official lake is Bassenthwaite Lake, as all the others are 'meres' or 'waters'. The longest lake is Windermere, at ten and a half miles, and the deepest, Wastwater at 243 feet.

Lanes near main A66

I pass through Threlkeld, which is a lovely looking town with the huge Blencathra (also known as the Saddleback, 868m), one of the most prominent fells in the northern Lake District rising up behind. I look up and can see tiny specs in red and blue coats moving slowly up the hillside.

Another trip idea is forming... Maybe I can get a few of the boys to come up and we do some walking, followed by some nice real ale in the great pubs in this area?

The landscape is really stunning now. Steep and shapely peaks are all around. The Lake District is definitely one of the best bits of the UK, just like Brecon but bigger and with more water.

I detour uphill and follow the signs for a stone circle. I wonder if it's worth it, especially as we have so many stone circles in Wales (one just a few hundred yards from my house in Pontypridd) but in fairness the Castlerigg Stone Circle is great - the Lake District's answer to Stone Henge.

Mountains

The circle itself is made of local metamorphic slate and this ancient site is particularly impressive because of its location; a natural amphitheatre surrounded by some of the highest peaks in the county: Helvellyn (950m), Skiddaw (931m), Grasmoor (852m) and Blencathra (868m).

The stone circle is thought to have been constructed about 3000 BC, making it one of the earliest in the country. Although there are more than 300 stone circles in Britain, the majority of them are from the Bronze Age and incorporate burial pits. These much earlier Neolithic circles, such as Castlerigg, do not contain formal burials.

There are thirty-eight stones, some of which are eight feet high. The stones stand in an oval shape, which is approximately 100 feet in diameter, with ten more stones shaped like a rectangle inside.

Blencathra

Information board

After the photo I whizz along a country lane, down a great hill and into the touristy town of Keswick. A quick text and I meet Sue and Lili, who has just had a run and play in Fitz Park, which is situated just a few minutes walk from the town centre in a lovely location beside the river Greta.

View from Castlerigg Stone Circle

We walk through town and discover it's packed. Thursdays must be market day unless of course it's just a summer event.

Keswick was inhabited in prehistoric times but the earliest reference is from the 13th Century when Edward I granted the town a charter for the market. Maybe that's why there are so many people here?

The town is also famous for poetry, being associated with Coleridge and Wordsworth, both of which put the area around the town and lakes on the map with their descriptions of its scenic beauty.

Of course for me the town is famous for another reason. The world's longest pencil lives in Keswick at the Pencil museum. The eight metre long implement features in the 2012 British horror comedy 'Sightseers', written and starring Alice Lowe and Steve Oram. I couldn't see anyone I fancied brutally murdering even though a group of loud Americans walked past so settled for a drink and some chips outside the Kings Arms instead.

Touristy Keswick

Keswick

Graphite was first discovered in the hills around Keswick in the 16th Century, and when the pencil was invented it led to the development of a massive industry in the Lake District. Today, the Cumberland Pencil Museum sits on the site of the original factory.

"Where's Eve?" I ask.

"Oh she's just tired and having a rest in the van."

"OK, I'll text her to see if she'll walk over for chips."

Eve replies to my text with, "What pub are you in?" and me and Sue wait, and wait…

Then she doesn't answer her phone, then we wonder where she is? Like any doting father I decide she's fine and cycle off leaving Sue to worry and Lili to continue to smell the myriad of dogs that are strolling past our table.

Bassenthwaite Lake – the only lake in the Lake District

I use the A66 out of town and soon find some trails. I decide to head for Cockermouth seeing as I'm a poet and Wordsworth was born there. Not sure why, just it seemed the right thing to do.

Cycling past Bassenthwaite Lake National Nature

Reserve I stop to take a photo. I also text Sue – no answer. Then I text Eve – no answer. Then I try ringing them both – answer machine. Oops.

Now I'm worried but eventually I get a reply that all's well and they just lost each other walking in circles around the town looking for each other. I learn later that they didn't even see the giant pencil.

Eventually I reach Cockermouth, home of the great nature poet. I find his house but they won't let me in unless I pay £9.50. I decline. It's not as if he could get me a publishing contract is it, being dead and everything.

Fletcher Christian came from near Cockermouth

Don't laugh but the town is named such because it is at the confluence of the River Cocker as it flows into the River Derwent. The word 'cocker' probably comes from the old Welsh for 'crooked one'.

The Romans built a fort nearby to protect the river crossing on a major route for troops heading towards Hadrian's Wall. The Normans built Cockermouth Castle but Robert the Bruce didn't like it so not much remains today.

It's a nice town though, long main street and well worth a visit. There is a pub named the Fletcher Christian, which alludes to the fact that the famous mutineer came from nearby Eaglesfield. After taking control of HMS Bounty he became an outlaw. Some accounts say the mutiny happened because of Bligh's harsh treatment of his men but others say it was the allure of the idyllic life and sexual favours of the Tahitian women – fair call I reckon.

William Wordsworth's house and museum

The mutineers that survived eventually landed at Pitcairn Island, burnt their ship and attempted to set up home on the island. The imbalance in numbers of men and women proved too much though and fights broke out that saw most of the men killed.

A US seal-hunting ship found John Adams (the last of the mutineers) still alive and living with nine Tahitian women. Yep, I know what you're thinking - the lucky, lucky b******!

There were numerous stories about how Mister Christian met his end although some say he faked his death and returned to England where his story inspired Coleridge to write 'The Rime of the Ancient Mariner'.

After leaving Cockermouth I took the road to Egremont and cut across country to save some miles. It appeared that most drivers had decided to do the same thing so I turned off when I got the chance, heading to Workington through country lanes and then eventually turning off when I saw signs to Whitehaven.

Ullock

I passed though a number of small and pretty villages, like Ullock and Brantwaite before joining a cycle trail near the main road.

I took one last look back at the lakes and wished we could stay longer, such is its beauty, before I started to recognise the cycle trails. I had gone full circle now as I remembered that a week ago I had cycled in the opposite direction on these same tracks when I'd left Ravenglass.

Lake District

Homeward bound

I knew I was close now yet the trails seemed to go up and down without ever actually getting me any closer to

Whitehaven and my final destination.

It was very sunny now and I stripped back to my one layer as I spotted Eve and Lili on the quayside, just across from the C2C sign.

Sunshine before the storm

I waved as I stopped, went down to the water's edge and dipped my front wheel in the Irish Sea (as is tradition apparently).

Described by Greenpeace and other environmental groups as the most radioactively contaminated sea in the world I soon regretted bringing all that plutonium onboard the campervan and hence back to Wales. Ah well, if my teeth fall out and I sprout an extra testicle I know what caused it.

It was really hot now and a great day to finish on. The forecast for tomorrow (Friday) was horrendous though so after I meet Sue we decide to just load up and head south in the van. Sue drives along the peninsular to the M6 and I sit in the back with the bike and Lili. I sip on a litre bottle of Stella to celebrate.

It's a bit of a rush and an anti-climax regards any

post-ride drinks but the weather is not looking good at all and knowing how easily the roads in Cumbria can flood (not to mention any additional curses we didn't know about) we make the right decision.

Whitehaven

Eve gives me a 'Well Done' card and a box of chocolates which I eat as we head home towards Wales.

*

The first part of the journey was fine and the weather OK but about the time we got near the M6 the rain and gales started.

Just like the Inuit people have lots of words for snow, the residents of Cumbria also have lots of words for rain, including 'mizzling' (drizzling rain), 'syling' (heavy rain), 'hossing' (slightly heavier rain), 'stotting (very heavy rain), and 'hoyin it doown' (really heavy rain).

It would be soon hoyin it doown.

Cycling Stats

Start: 8:30am
Distance: 47.57 miles
Total Distance: 274.38 miles
Average Speed: 10.2 mph
Fastest Speed: 31.4 mph
Cycling Time: 8 hrs 19 mins
Finish: 6:00pm
Calories: 3459
Ascent: 710m
Descent: 846m
Beers: 1

Route

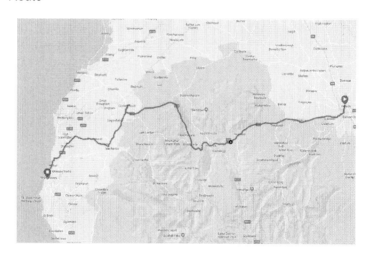

Hill Profile

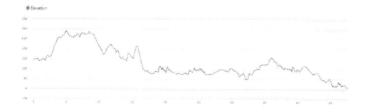

 Day 8

Whitehaven to Pontypridd
Friday 9th August 2019

CD music: Wild is the Wind – David Bowie

We stopped for a McDonalds just past midnight at one of the motorway services. Eve had two meals and Lili looked on longingly. We hit more severe rain and wind not long after and by the time we approached Birmingham we'd aquaplaned a few times in the van. Chirpy Carol Kirkwood was right for once.

The beautiful Lake District a distant memory already

Then I took the wrong turning (or at least I saw the right lane far too late and had to just carry on for fearing of taking a car out) and we sort of headed for the NEC. Oops.

"Quick, any phones got charge left?"

"Your iPhone is dead dad," says Eve, helpfully.

"Bloody hell, I can't remember my midlands geography..."

"My iPhone is crap too," adds Eve.

"What about mam's?"

"Yeh, that's got 10% on."

So a quick chat to the nice woman on Google Maps (who we call Sharon) and a few lane changes, roundabouts and we're on the M42 for a bit before finding our way back to the M5.

"Thank Dawkins for that," I say with relief.

"More Boost juice dad?"

"Yep."

I carry on driving through the night and actually drive all the way home to Pontypridd as for some reason I didn't feel tired at all. Maybe I could have done that extra twenty miles after all? Maybe drinking a litre of 'Boost' energy drink is not good for your kidneys? Time will tell.

Statistics

Day	Distance (Miles)	Average Speed (mph)
1	30.53	10.3
2	57.84	11.4
3	47.15	10.9
4	45.28	9.2
5	46.01	8.7
6	47.57	10.2
Total	**274.38**	**10.1**

Metres climbed: 3,196
Calories used: 18,865

Starting weight: 103kg
Finishing weight: 95kg

So a good workout and a great diet plan ☺

Pros and Cons

Although to many cyclists 300 miles is only a couple of days on a bike (probably just one for legend Mark Beaumont) and the fact we had to cut the 'Roman Holiday' short due to the incoming weather meant I only managed 274 miles, I still think that this is the way to go for me in the future. Over the six days I still averaged forty-five miles per day cycling so not too bad I guess.

Firstly, I'm just not that fit. And carrying sixteen stone around at fifty-three I have to be careful. But secondly, and more importantly for me, I think seeing more things and enjoying the route, the sights, the wildlife and the people is a far more enjoyable way to spend my time. In fact, for my next trip I think I might even set a maximum of thirty miles per day so I can have a few beers in the night and not worry about getting up too early the next day.

OK, the good bits and bad bits if you're thinking about doing a similar ride:

The *Hadrian's Cycleway* is awesome. It's well-signposted, easy to follow and even if you get lost you just cut across a few country lanes or even the main A roads and you'll soon pick it up again. There are not too many hills although the ones there are are quite nasty. You cycle right next to the famous wall and also right into the heart of the great cities of Newcastle and Sunderland. I also loved Tynemouth on the coast although it tipped down with rain when I arrived. I might have been helped along by tailwinds but didn't really notice any to be honest.

The *C2C* I didn't find as good but that was probably because I went against the flow (prevailing SW winds) and hit a bugger of a headwind on the Pennines. I reckon going the other way though would be great and I was passed by many cyclists literally speeding along the trail going west to east.

The scenery in County Durham was amazing as were the lakes. The best bit though? And I don't say this often - the people. Everyone we met was friendly and so helpful, so to our friends in the north, thank you for making a great trip even better.

Regrets? Yes Frank, a few, one my fault and one out of my control. My confusion between Sustrans and Google Maps with the distances to Carlisle meant I missed going right around the coast although a passerby said there's not much to see there. And of course the weather reports meant I made use of a lift to cut off twenty miles on the last day, which I'd have preferred not to have done.

In conclusion though it was a great trip, I still like going clockwise, must be something about my in-built sexual magnetism aligning itself with the Earth and would highly recommend both the routes.

If you have a long week to spare then why not give it a go? I'm sure you'll love it.

Websites

Although not the greatest planner I did think it best if I check out any potential hazards I might encounter on the ride. A glance at the Sustrans website, zooming in and out quickly made me realise that crossing the River Tyne was something I needed to investigate.

www.sustrans.org.uk/find-a-route-on-the-national-cycle-network/hadrians-cycleway/

www.sustrans.org.uk/find-a-route-on-the-national-cycle-network/c2c-or-sea-to-sea/

When I realised the Tyne tunnel was closed due to asbestos I emailed Sustrans North-East and was told by the very kind Claire that I could get the Shields ferry from North Shields to South Shields and cycle down to Sunderland from there – so problem solved.

I also looked at the colour coding to see if the routes were on or off road.

Apart from that though I did very little research and decided it best to do that as I went along. A bit like my training.

Of course having done the ride I now see that having a few facts at my fingertips might have made for a better or at least slightly more informed and efficient trip. With this in mind I've included some resources for anyone following in my *pedals*.

I suppose it goes without saying but having access to a smartphone with Google Maps is essential these days because no matter who you are you're bound to get lost sometimes and it helps to know that Google, Apple, the CIA, NSA, MI5, GCHQ and so on have your back.

In my case this was a lifesaver but as a result of this

trip I have now decided to ditch Apple and my state-of-the-art iPhone 5 (yeh I know, an old model) and go for a mobile that actually has a battery in it that will last a day of being used. I'm looking at getting a Moto G7 Power as the reviews say it has the best battery life (at time of writing of course).

As for a guidebook or maps, as much as I love them both, personally, I wouldn't bother as they just add extra weight but maybe a novel or history book of the area might help to pass the time or cheer you up if you ever get stranded in Washington ☺

Useful sites:

www.ravenglass-railway.co.uk

www.newscientist.com/article/mg22530053-800-shocking-state-of-worlds-riskiest-nuclear-waste-site

www.visit-whitehaven.co.uk

www.gale-brow-caravan-and-camping-site.business.site

www.oilyspub.co.uk

www.irthingvalecaravanpark.co.uk

www.hadrianswallcountry.co.uk

www.english-heritage.org.uk/visit/places/lanercost-priory

www.english-heritage.org.uk/visit/places/corbridge-roman-town-hadrians-wall

www.nhsn.ncl.ac.uk/activities/conservation-research/tyne-kittiwakes

www.sunderlandculture.org.uk/our-venues/national-glass-centre

www.beamish.org.uk

www.northpennines.org.uk

www.parkheadstation.co.uk

www.killhope.org.uk

www.visitcumbria.com/evnp/nenthead

www.discoverpenrith.co.uk

www.lakedistrict.gov.uk

www.keswick.org

www.derwentart.com

www.cockermouth.org.uk

And lastly I suppose I should also mention *DuckDuckGo* that I used (instead of *Evil Google*) to check my facts with regards the towns and history stuff when writing this account up.

Dave Lewis is from Cilfynydd, South Wales. He has always lived in Wales except for a year in Kenya.

He has published a number of books to date, and this is his third cycling book.

Please pass this book on to anyone who fancies jumping on a bike to do the same ride, because it's a great ride with plenty of history and you're sure to meet some lovely people along the way.

Also, if you liked this book and could find five minutes to leave a positive review on Amazon, Dave would be thrilled.

And finally, good luck to anyone that does the ride – we hope you have as much fun as we did.

For more information about the author and to see his other work please visit his web site – www.david-lewis.co.uk

By the same author:

Poetry:
Layer Cake © 2009
Urban Birdsong © 2010
Sawing Fallen Logs For Ladybird Houses © 2011
Haiku © 2012
Roadkill © 2013
Reclaiming The Beat © 2016
Going Off Grid © 2018
Never Seventeen © 2018

Novels:
Ctrl-Alt-Delete © 2011
Raising Skinny Elephants © 2013
iCommand © 2015

Edited:
Welsh Poetry Competition Anthology © 2011
Welsh Poetry Competition Anthology II © 2016

Non-Fiction:
Photography Composition © 2014
Land's End to John o' Groats © 2015
Wales Trails © 2016
Happy © 2017
Basic Photoshop © 2017

Websites:
www.david-lewis.co.uk
www.wales-trails.co.uk
www.welshpoetry.co.uk
www.publishandprint.co.uk
www.welshwriters.co.uk

Printed in Great Britain
by Amazon